Alberta D. Jones

SPACE INVADERS INFINITY GENE EVOLVE

GAME GUIDE

Unlocking the Full Evolution Experience

Chapter 1: Introduction to Space Invaders Infinity Gene Evolve

1.1 Overview of the Game

Space Invaders Infinity Gene Evolve is the latest installment in the legendary **Space Invaders** franchise, exclusively launching on **Apple Arcade**. It builds upon the revolutionary mechanics of **Space Invaders Infinity Gene (2009)**, evolving the gameplay from classic 2D arcade action into a dynamically shifting shooter with modern visuals and mechanics.

Key Features:

- **Evolutionary Gameplay:** The game starts with traditional Space Invaders-style gameplay but evolves over time, introducing new weapons, ships, and 3D transformations.
- **Expansive Weaponry:** Players unlock an arsenal of weapons, from simple laser shots to devastating area-of-effect attacks.
- **Guest Ships:** Features iconic ships from **TAITO's** shooter lineup, including **Darius, Night Striker, and RayStorm**.
- **Multiple Game Modes:** Play through **Classic Mode**, **Evolution Mode**, **Survival**, and various **Challenge Modes**.
- **Dynamic Enemy Behavior:** Alien invaders adapt to your playstyle, making each playthrough unique.
- **Immersive Visuals & Soundtrack:** A mesmerizing blend of **retro aesthetics and futuristic neon-infused graphics**,

accompanied by an **electronic soundtrack** that evolves alongside the gameplay.

Gameplay Concept:

Players begin with a simple spaceship and engage in wave-based battles against alien invaders. As they progress, the game "evolves" by introducing **new mechanics, ship abilities, enemy types, and 3D space movement**, transforming a basic arcade shooter into a high-speed **bullet hell experience**.

This evolution mechanic makes **Space Invaders Infinity Gene Evolve** stand out from traditional Space Invaders games, keeping players engaged with continuous progression and increasing complexity.

1.2 Evolution from Classic to Modern Gameplay

From Arcade Simplicity to Dynamic Evolution

The original **Space Invaders (1978)** was a simple yet addictive fixed shooter where players controlled a laser cannon to destroy waves of descending aliens. Over the decades, various sequels and spin-offs introduced new mechanics, but **Space Invaders Infinity Gene (2009)** revolutionized the series by introducing a dynamic evolution system that transformed gameplay as players progressed.

Space Invaders Infinity Gene Evolve builds upon this concept, pushing it further with **modern 3D graphics, adaptive gameplay, and new interactive mechanics**, making it a blend of **classic arcade action and futuristic shoot-'em-up chaos**.

Stages of Evolution

The game starts in a familiar **classic arcade mode**, mimicking the original **Space Invaders** experience. However, as players continue, the game **evolves** in several ways:

1. Gameplay Evolution

- **Classic 2D Shooter:** The game begins in a traditional fixed-screen style, where the player's ship moves left and right to shoot incoming enemies.
- **Scrolling Levels:** Instead of being confined to a single screen, levels begin to scroll horizontally and vertically, adding movement freedom.
- **Bullet Hell Mechanics:** Enemy fire patterns become more complex, requiring precision dodging.
- **3D Environments:** Later stages introduce **full 3D movement**, shifting from a flat shooter into a dynamic **space battle experience**.

2. Ship Evolution

- Players start with a **basic laser-firing ship**.
- As they progress, new **weapons, ships, and power-ups** become available.
- Guest ships from **TAITO classics like Darius and RayStorm** introduce unique playstyles.
- **Special abilities like homing shots, beam attacks, and rapid-fire lasers** allow for customized combat strategies.

3. Enemy Evolution

- Early enemies resemble the **classic alien invaders**, moving in predictable patterns.
- As the game progresses, they develop **new movement behaviors**, **advanced attack formations**, and **evasive maneuvers**.
- Boss fights introduce **gigantic, multi-phase enemies** that test reflexes and strategy.

Blending Retro and Modern Gaming

The gradual evolution from **classic arcade action to high-speed, dynamic shoot-'em-up gameplay** makes **Space Invaders Infinity Gene Evolve** an engaging experience. By blending **nostalgic elements** with **modern mechanics**, the game caters to both **longtime fans and newcomers** to the series.

1.3 Key Features and What's New

Space Invaders Infinity Gene Evolve builds upon the mechanics of **Space Invaders Infinity Gene (2009)** and introduces **new features, modern visuals, and expanded gameplay mechanics**. The game retains its **evolutionary gameplay concept** while enhancing every aspect of the experience.

Key Features

1. Evolutionary Gameplay System

- The game **starts in classic 2D Space Invaders style** but gradually evolves into a **dynamic shoot-'em-up** with scrolling backgrounds and **3D movement**.

- Players unlock **new weapons, abilities, and gameplay mechanics** as they progress.

- The visual style evolves, transforming from **retro pixel art** into **modern neon-infused graphics**.

2. Expansive Ship and Weapon Customization

- Players can **unlock and pilot different ships**, each with **unique abilities and weapons**.

- Features **guest ships from classic TAITO games** like **Darius, Night Striker, and RayStorm**.

- **Multiple weapon loadouts**, including **homing lasers, spread shots, beam cannons, and explosive rounds**.

3. Intense Enemy Encounters and Boss Battles

- Enemies **adapt and evolve**, using **new formations and attack patterns** as players progress.

- **Boss fights feature massive, multi-phase enemies** with unique mechanics.

- New enemy types introduced beyond the **classic Space Invaders aliens**.

4. Multiple Game Modes for Replayability

- **Classic Mode** – Experience the original **Space Invaders-style** gameplay.

- **Evolution Mode** – Unlocks new mechanics and ship upgrades.

- **Survival Mode** – Test endurance against endless waves of enemies.

- **Score Attack Mode** – Compete for **high scores** with limited resources.

- **Special Events and Challenges** – Limited-time events offering unique rewards.

5. Stunning Visuals and Adaptive Soundtrack

- **Smooth 60FPS gameplay** for a fluid and immersive experience.

- The **art style evolves,** from **minimalist retro graphics to futuristic 3D designs**.

- A **dynamic electronic soundtrack** that changes based on gameplay intensity.

What's New in Space Invaders Infinity Gene Evolve?

- **Enhanced Graphics & 3D Transformations** – Unlike the 2009 version, the game fully transitions into a **3D space shooter** in later stages.

- **Improved Enemy AI & Bullet Hell Mechanics** – Enemies now **adapt to player tactics**, making each run unique.

- **New Ships & TAITO Guest Fighters** – Unlockable ships from classic **TAITO shooters** provide **unique playstyles**.

- **Soundtrack Evolution** – The game's **music shifts dynamically** to match the intensity of battles.

- **Online Leaderboards & Challenges** – Compete globally with **scoreboards and timed events**.

1.4 Platforms and Availability

Available Platforms

Space Invaders Infinity Gene Evolve is an **Apple Arcade exclusive**, meaning it is only available on **Apple devices**. The game supports:

- **iPhone** (iOS)

- **iPad** (iPadOS)

- **Mac** (macOS)

- **Apple TV** (tvOS)

There are currently no announced plans for a **PC, console, or Android** release

Apple Arcade Subscription Requirement

Since the game is part of **Apple Arcade**, players must have an active **Apple Arcade subscription** to access it.

Apple Arcade Subscription Details:

- Monthly fee with a **free trial** for new users.

- No ads, in-app purchases, or paywalls.

- Access to a large library of **exclusive Apple Arcade games**.

- Supports **Family Sharing**, allowing up to six family members to play.

Release Date

Space Invaders Infinity Gene Evolve is set to launch on **April 3, 2025**, exclusively on Apple Arcade.

Controller Support and Cross-Device Play

- Supports **touchscreen controls** on iPhone and iPad.

- **Controller compatibility** for a more traditional console-like experience.

- **Cloud saves** allow seamless gameplay across **iPhone, iPad, Mac, and Apple TV**.

How to Download

1. Open the **App Store** on an Apple device.

2. Search for **Space Invaders Infinity Gene Evolve**.

3. Tap **"Get"** and install the game.

4. Launch the game through **Apple Arcade**.

Since the game is part of **Apple Arcade**, it cannot be purchased separately.

Chapter 2: Getting Started

2.1 System Requirements & Installation

System Requirements

Since **Space Invaders Infinity Gene Evolve** is an **Apple Arcade exclusive**, it is only available on **Apple devices**. Below are the system requirements for each platform.

iPhone & iPad

- **Operating System:** iOS 15.0 or later (recommended iOS 16+ for optimal performance).

- **Compatible Devices:**

  - iPhone 8 and newer.

  - iPad (5th generation and newer).

  - iPad Air (3rd generation and newer).

  - iPad Pro (all models).

- **Storage Space:** At least **2 GB of free space** is recommended.

- **Processor:** A12 Bionic chip or newer for the best gameplay experience.

- **Controller Support:** Compatible with **Bluetooth controllers**, including **PS5 DualSense, Xbox, and MFi controllers**.

Mac

- **Operating System:** macOS 12 Monterey or later.

- **Processor:** Apple M1 chip or newer (Intel Core i5 supported but may experience performance issues).

- **RAM:** Minimum **4 GB RAM**, but **8 GB recommended** for smooth gameplay.

- **Storage Space:** At least **2 GB of free space**.

- **Graphics:** Apple's integrated GPU or an equivalent discrete GPU.

- **Controller Support:** Compatible with **USB and Bluetooth controllers** for an enhanced experience.

Apple TV

- **Operating System:** tvOS 15 or later.

- **Compatible Devices:**

    ○ Apple TV HD (2015 and later).

    ○ Apple TV 4K (1st generation and newer).

- **Controller Support:** Fully compatible with **Apple Arcade-certified controllers**, including **Xbox and PlayStation controllers**.

Installation Guide

Since **Space Invaders Infinity Gene Evolve** is part of **Apple Arcade**, the installation process is simple and requires an **active Apple Arcade subscription**.

Steps to Install on iPhone & iPad

1. Open the **App Store** on your device.

2. Tap on the **Arcade** tab at the bottom of the screen.

3. Use the search bar and type "**Space Invaders Infinity Gene Evolve**".

4. Select the game from the search results.

5. Tap **Get** or the **download button** to install the game.

6. Wait for the installation to complete, then tap **Open** to start playing.

Steps to Install on Mac

1. Open the **App Store** from the Dock or Applications folder.

2. Click on the **Arcade** tab in the App Store.

3. Search for **"Space Invaders Infinity Gene Evolve"**.

4. Click **Get** or the **download button**.

5. Once the installation is complete, open the game from the **Applications folder** or **Launchpad**.

Steps to Install on Apple TV

1. Open the **App Store** on your Apple TV.

2. Navigate to the **Arcade** section.

3. Use the search function to find **"Space Invaders Infinity Gene Evolve"**.

4. Select the game and click **Get** to start downloading.

5. Once installed, open the game from your home screen.

Subscription Requirement

Since **Space Invaders Infinity Gene Evolve** is exclusive to **Apple Arcade**, you must have an **active Apple Arcade subscription** to play.

- **New users** can get a **one-month free trial**.

- **Apple Arcade costs $4.99/month** after the trial.

- **Family Sharing** allows up to **six family members** to play under one subscription.

Cloud Saves and Cross-Device Play

Apple Arcade supports **iCloud game saves**, allowing you to **continue your progress across multiple Apple devices**.

- Start playing on **iPhone** and continue on **Mac or Apple TV**.

- Game progress is automatically synced via **iCloud**.

- Ensure you are signed into the **same Apple ID** on all devices for seamless gameplay.

2.2 Navigating the Main Menu

Upon launching **Space Invaders Infinity Gene Evolve**, players are greeted with the **main menu**, which serves as the central hub for all game options. The interface is designed to be intuitive, with a clean, futuristic aesthetic that evolves as the player progresses.

Main Menu Layout and Options

The main menu consists of several key sections, each providing access to different game modes, settings, and customization features.

1. Start Game

- This option begins a **new game** or continues a **previous session** from the last save point.

- If a saved game exists, players can choose to:

  - **Continue** – Resume from the last checkpoint.

  - **New Game** – Start fresh, resetting progress while keeping unlocked features.

2. Game Modes

- **Classic Mode** – Traditional **Space Invaders** gameplay with minimal evolution.

- **Evolution Mode** – The full experience, featuring progressive gameplay evolution.

- **Survival Mode** – Endless waves of enemies with increasing difficulty.

- **Score Attack Mode** – Compete for high scores in timed challenges.

- **Event Challenges** – Special limited-time challenges with unique objectives.

3. Ship Customization

- Players can choose from **unlocked ships**, each with different attributes.

- Loadouts can be customized with **various weapons, shields, and upgrades**.

- Guest ships from **TAITO's classic franchises** can be selected if unlocked.

4. Settings

- **Controls** – Adjust touch controls, controller sensitivity, and button mapping.

- **Graphics** – Toggle between standard and high-performance visual modes.

- **Audio** – Adjust background music, sound effects, and voice levels.

- **Accessibility** – Enable features like colorblind modes and screen shake reduction.

5. Leaderboards & Achievements

- Displays **global rankings** for Score Attack and Survival modes.

- Tracks **in-game milestones and trophies**.

- Syncs with **Game Center** for online leaderboard access.

6. Extras & Bonus Content

- **Gallery** – View concept art, unlocked skins, and retro arcade materials.

- **Music Player** – Listen to the game's evolving soundtrack.

- **TAITO Legacy Section** – Explore classic **TAITO history and references**.

7. Exit/Quit

- Allows players to return to the **Apple Arcade dashboard** or close the game.

How the Menu Evolves

As players progress, the main menu **transforms visually** to reflect their achievements:

- **Classic Start** – Simple monochrome pixelated style.

- **Evolving State** – Gradual introduction of neon colors and animated effects.

- **Advanced Progression** – Full 3D animated visuals with reactive background effects.

2.3 Game Modes Explained

Space Invaders Infinity Gene Evolve offers multiple game modes, each designed to provide a unique gameplay experience. These modes range from a **traditional arcade style** to **evolutionary gameplay** that transforms over time.

1. Classic Mode

This mode replicates the **original Space Invaders experience** while incorporating smoother controls and minor enhancements.

Features:

- Traditional **2D arcade gameplay** with basic enemy waves.

- Limited weapon variety—players can only use the **classic laser cannon**.

- Fixed movement—players can only move left and right at the bottom of the screen.

- Score-based progression with extra lives gained at certain point thresholds.

- Pixel-art **retro visuals** reminiscent of the 1978 original.

Best For:

- Players who enjoy **nostalgic arcade gameplay**.

- Those who want a **simplified, challenge-based experience**.

2. Evolution Mode *(Main Story Mode)*

This is the **primary mode** where the game evolves as the player progresses. It starts in **Classic Mode style** but gradually **introduces modern mechanics**.

Features:

- Begins with **basic movement and shooting** but evolves into **free movement and advanced weaponry**.

- New enemy types and **adaptive AI that changes attack patterns**.

- **Graphical evolution** – From simple black-and-white visuals to fully animated neon 3D effects.

- **Multiple ship forms and unlockable abilities**, including homing lasers, rapid-fire weapons, and shields.

- Stage-based progression with increasing difficulty and **boss battles**.

Best For:

- Players looking for a **progressive gameplay experience**.

- Those who want a **blend of classic and modern gameplay mechanics**.

3. Survival Mode *(Endless Mode)*

A fast-paced **endurance challenge** where players must survive against **increasingly difficult waves** of enemies.

Features:

- No level progression—players **face endless waves** of enemies until they lose all lives.

- Enemies **become faster and more aggressive** over time.

- Players can pick up **random power-ups** but have limited resources.

- **Leaderboard integration** for global rankings.

Best For:

- Competitive players looking to **test their reflexes and endurance**.

- Those who enjoy **high-score chasing**.

4. Score Attack Mode *(Timed Challenges)*

A **competitive mode** where players attempt to earn the **highest score possible within a set time limit**.

Features:

- Time-limited stages where players must defeat **as many enemies as possible**.

- **Multiplier mechanics** – Chaining enemy kills increases score multipliers.

- Limited lives and weapons, requiring **strategic play**.

- **Online leaderboards** to compare high scores with other players.

Best For:

- Players who enjoy **arcade-style scoring challenges**.

- Competitive gamers aiming for **global high scores**.

5. Event Challenges *(Limited-Time Special Modes)*

These **rotating events** introduce **unique rules** and **special enemies** not found in other modes.

Features:

- Time-limited **weekly or seasonal challenges**.

- **Unique boss fights** and experimental mechanics.

- Special rewards like **alternate ship designs and weapon skins**.

- Some events **feature guest content from classic TAITO games**.

Best For:

- Players who enjoy **fresh, rotating challenges**.

- Those looking for **exclusive unlockables and rewards**.

2.4 Basic Controls & Customization

Understanding the controls in **Space Invaders Infinity Gene Evolve** is essential for mastering the game. The game supports **touchscreen controls, controller support**, and **customization options** to suit different playstyles.

Basic Controls

Touchscreen Controls (iPhone & iPad)

For players using an **iPhone or iPad**, the game provides an **intuitive touch-based control system**:

Action	Touchscreen Control
Move Ship	Swipe left or right (Classic Mode) / Swipe freely (Evolution Mode)
Shoot	Tap anywhere on the screen

Autofire	Hold finger on the screen
Special Weapon	Two-finger tap
Bomb (if available)	Three-finger tap
Pause Game	Tap the pause button (top corner)

Touch Sensitivity: The game allows players to adjust **touch sensitivity** in the settings to fine-tune movement speed.

Controller Controls (Mac, Apple TV, iOS with Bluetooth Controllers)

For players using a **Bluetooth or USB controller**, the controls are mapped similarly to a **console-style shooter**.

Action	PlayStation Controller	Xbox Controller	Apple/MFi Controller
Move Ship	Left Stick or D-Pad	Left Stick or D-Pad	Left Stick or D-Pad
Shoot	X / Square	A / X	A
Autofire	Hold X / Square	Hold A / X	Hold A
Special Weapon	Triangle	Y	Y

Bomb (if available)	Circle	B	B
Pause	Options Button	Menu Button	Pause Button

Controller Vibration: Players can enable or disable **controller vibration feedback** in the settings.

Keyboard Controls (Mac Only)

For those playing on **Mac**, the game allows keyboard input.

Action	Default Key
Move Ship	Arrow Keys or WASD
Shoot	Spacebar
Autofire	Hold Spacebar
Special Weapon	Shift
Bomb (if available)	Ctrl or Command
Pause	Esc or P

Control Customization

Players can customize the control layout in the **Settings Menu** under the **Controls** tab.

Customization Options:

- **Rebind Keys/Buttons:** Allows remapping of movement, shooting, and special abilities.

- **Touch Sensitivity Adjustment:** Adjusts how fast the ship moves when swiping.

- **Autofire Toggle:** Enables/disables continuous shooting when holding the button.

- **Invert Controls:** Allows inversion of movement or aim if needed.

- **Controller Vibration:** Enables/disables controller rumble feedback.

Chapter 3: Understanding the Evolution System

3.1 How Evolution Works

The **Evolution System** in *Space Invaders Infinity Gene Evolve* dynamically changes the gameplay experience as players progress. The game starts with **classic arcade mechanics**, but as players defeat enemies and clear levels, the gameplay **evolves**, introducing new **movement mechanics, weapons, enemy behaviors, and visual transformations.**

Key Aspects of Evolution

1. **Gradual Gameplay Expansion**

   - Initially, movement is **limited to left and right** (like the original *Space Invaders*).

   - As the game evolves, players **gain full directional movement**, adding new layers of strategy.

   - Weapons start with a simple **single-shot laser**, but as evolution progresses, **homing missiles, spread shots, and charge beams** become available.

2. **Environmental and Visual Changes**

   - Early levels feature **minimalist retro graphics** similar to the 1978 original.

- As evolution occurs, the backgrounds become more **detailed and dynamic**, shifting from **2D pixel art to animated neon 3D environments**.

3. **Adaptive Enemy AI and Patterns**

    - At first, enemies **move in simple patterns** like in the classic game.

    - As the game evolves, enemies **become faster, more aggressive, and use complex attack formations**.

    - Boss fights **increase in complexity**, introducing **multi-phase battles and bullet-hell mechanics**.

4. **Music and Soundtrack Evolution**

    - Early levels feature **chiptune-style music** similar to classic arcade games.

    - As evolution progresses, the soundtrack **adds more instruments, depth, and dynamic effects**, aligning with the game's evolving nature.

How to Trigger Evolution

- **Clearing Levels:** Completing stages naturally progresses the evolution system.

- **Score Milestones:** Achieving high scores unlocks new mechanics faster.

- **Defeating Bosses:** Boss fights mark major evolutionary shifts in gameplay.

- **Collecting Evolution Points (EP):** Some stages reward **Evolution Points**, which unlock upgrades and new abilities.

3.2 Unlocking New Features and Weapons

As the game evolves, players gain access to **new features, power-ups, and weapons** that drastically change combat.

Key Unlockable Features

Feature	How to Unlock	Effect
Free Movement	Stage 3 Evolution	Allows movement in all directions.
Weapon Customization	Stage 5 Evolution	Unlocks different ship loadouts and weapon choices.
Special Abilities	Score milestones	Adds special attacks like shields and time-slowing.
Stage Select Mode	Complete Evolution Mode	Lets players replay any stage.
Color Themes	Hidden achievements	Allows customization of HUD and visuals.

New Weapons & Power-Ups

Weapon	Effect	How to Unlock
Spread Shot	Fires multiple projectiles in different directions.	Mid-stage evolution.
Homing Missiles	Auto-targets enemies.	High-score bonus.
Charge Beam	Fires a powerful blast after charging.	Evolution Level 4.
Wave Cannon	Penetrates multiple enemies.	Defeat a mid-game boss.
Shield Generator	Absorbs one enemy attack.	Stage reward.

3.3 Stages of Evolution: 2D to 3D Transition

One of the most exciting aspects of *Space Invaders Infinity Gene Evolve* is its **gradual transformation from a classic 2D arcade shooter into a fully dynamic 3D experience**. This shift occurs over multiple evolution stages, altering everything from gameplay mechanics to visual presentation.

Evolutionary Stages

1. **Stage 1: Classic 2D Arcade Style**

- The game begins with the **original 1978-inspired mechanics**.

- Players can only move **left and right** at the bottom of the screen.

- Simple **black-and-white pixel visuals** with a static background.

- Single-shot **laser weapon**, similar to the original.

2. **Stage 2: Expanded 2D Movement**

- Unlocks **vertical movement**, allowing more freedom to dodge attacks.

- Introduces **new enemy formations** that require different strategies.

- Color enhancements and **dynamic background effects** begin appearing.

- Weapons evolve, adding **faster shooting** and **early power-ups**.

3. **Stage 3: Pseudo-3D Perspective (Isometric View)**

- The camera shifts slightly, adding **depth to the environment**.

- Enemies start **emerging from the background**, attacking from multiple angles.

- New weapons like homing missiles and charge beams become available.

- The game's speed increases, introducing **faster dodging and reaction-based gameplay**.

4. **Stage 4: Full 3D Gameplay**

- The game fully transitions into a **3D bullet-hell style shooter**.

- Players can move **freely in all directions**, dodging waves of projectiles.

- Enemy AI becomes **adaptive**, reacting to player movement.

- Graphics shift to **dynamic neon and holographic effects**, creating an intense futuristic atmosphere.

5. **Stage 5: Advanced Evolution (Full Space Combat Feel)**

- Players can now experience **360-degree movement**, similar to modern space shooters.

- **Enemies attack from all directions**, requiring full situational awareness.

- **Boss fights become multi-phased**, featuring rotating arenas and destructible environments.

- **Ultimate weapons** like the **Wave Cannon** and **Multi-Laser** are unlocked.

Visual and Sound Evolution

- The **music changes dynamically**, shifting from simple beeps to an orchestrated electronic soundtrack.

- Particle effects, glowing neon trails, and **motion blur effects** enhance the futuristic feel.

- Older elements are **still present but reimagined**, keeping nostalgia alive while embracing modern gameplay.

3.4 Managing Upgrades Effectively

As the game evolves, managing upgrades becomes essential for **survival and efficiency**. Players must decide which **weapons, ship enhancements, and abilities** to prioritize based on their playstyle.

Key Upgrade Categories

Upgrade Type	Effect	Best For
Weapon Enhancements	Increases fire rate, damage, or range of attacks.	Aggressive players who focus on eliminating enemies quickly.
Ship Speed & Maneuverability	Improves movement speed and dodging capability.	Players who prefer speed-based dodging rather than shields.
Defensive Shields	Provides temporary invincibility or absorbs attacks.	Those who struggle with bullet-hell mechanics.

Special Abilities	Unlocks powerful tools like slow-motion or area-clearing bombs.	Players who want additional strategic options.

Best Upgrade Strategies

1. **Balance Offense and Defense**

   - While stronger weapons help eliminate enemies quickly, investing in **defensive upgrades** can prevent unnecessary deaths.

2. **Adapt to the Stage Design**

   - Some levels favor **wide-range weapons** like spread shots, while others require **precision weapons** like charge beams.

   - Speed upgrades are crucial for **bullet-heavy sections**, while shields can help against **aggressive bosses**.

3. **Experiment with Loadouts**

   - Different **weapon combinations** work better for different enemy types.

   - Testing multiple setups helps find the best **balance between attack power and mobility**.

4. **Upgrade Based on Game Mode**

    ○   In **Survival Mode**, prioritize **shields and movement speed**.

    ○   In **Score Attack**, focus on **high-damage, rapid-fire weapons**.

    ○   In **Evolution Mode**, a **balanced approach** ensures smoother progression.

Chapter 4: Ship Selection and Customization

4.1 Default Ship and Its Capabilities

Overview of the Default Ship

The **Standard Fighter** is the starting ship in the game, designed for balanced gameplay. It retains a **classic Space Invaders aesthetic**, gradually evolving as the player progresses.

Key Features:

- **Balanced Speed & Mobility:** Moderate movement speed allows for precision dodging.

- **Basic Laser Weapon:** Fires single shots at a steady pace, similar to the original *Space Invaders*.

- **Upgrade Potential:** Gains access to **movement improvements, faster fire rate, and advanced weapons** as the game evolves.

- **No Special Abilities Initially:** Unlike later ships, the default fighter doesn't start with special attacks or shields.

Pros & Cons:

Pros	Cons
Well-balanced for beginners	Starts with a weak single-shot laser
Easy to control	Lacks special abilities at the start
Evolves steadily into a stronger fighter	Limited movement range in early stages

4.2 Unlocking and Using Guest Fighters

As players progress, they can unlock **special ships** inspired by **classic TAITO arcade games**. These **guest fighters** bring unique weapons, movement patterns, and abilities that drastically alter gameplay.

How to Unlock Guest Fighters:

- **High Scores & Achievements:** Some ships unlock when players reach specific score milestones.

- **Completing Stages:** Certain guest fighters become available after **defeating major bosses** or completing evolution stages.

- **Limited-Time Events:** Some ships are only available through special challenges or events.

Notable Guest Fighters:

Ship Name	Game of Origin	Unique Ability
Silver Hawk	*Darius*	Uses wave beam and homing missiles
R-Gray 1	*RayForce*	Features a powerful lock-on laser
Metal Black Ship	*Metal Black*	Can absorb enemy energy to charge a special attack
XEXEX Fighter	*XEXEX*	Has a detachable energy pod for extra firepower
Arkanoid Vaus	*Arkanoid*	Shoots bouncing energy balls instead of lasers

Each guest fighter plays differently, offering **unique attack styles, movement physics, and strategic options**.

4.3 Weapon Loadouts and Their Effects

Each ship can equip different **weapon loadouts**, affecting firepower, range, and effectiveness in combat. Choosing the right loadout can mean the difference between **survival and defeat** in later stages.

Primary Weapon Types:

Weapon	Effect	Best For
Single Laser	Standard straight shot	Beginners, early levels
Spread Shot	Fires multiple bullets in a wide arc	Swarm enemies, crowd control
Homing Missiles	Seeks out enemies automatically	Fast-moving enemies
Charge Beam	Requires charging but deals massive damage	Boss fights
Wave Cannon	Pierces through multiple enemies	Large enemy formations

Secondary Weapons & Power-Ups:

Secondary Weapon	Effect
Side Lasers	Adds extra lasers shooting from both sides
Homing Orbs	Small energy balls that track enemies
Plasma Shield	Absorbs one enemy attack before breaking
Time-Slowing Device	Temporarily slows enemy movement

Energy Absorption	Converts enemy shots into health or score bonuses

Selecting the right combination of **primary and secondary weapons** can give players an edge in different game modes.

4.4 Best Ships for Different Playstyles

Each ship has strengths and weaknesses, making some better suited for **certain playstyles and game modes**.

Recommended Ships by Playstyle:

Playstyle	Best Ship	Why?
Balanced (All-Rounder)	**Default Ship**	Well-rounded stats, evolves steadily
Aggressive Attacker	**R-Gray 1 (RayForce)**	Lock-on laser quickly eliminates enemies
Speed & Evasion	**XEXEX Fighter**	Fast movement, energy pod adds extra firepower
Defensive & Strategic	**Arkanoid Vaus**	Reflective energy shots provide unique attack style
High-Score Chaser	**Silver Hawk (Darius)**	Wide attack range and homing missiles increase score potential

Players should experiment with different ships to find the one that best fits their **reflexes, strategy, and preferred playstyle**.

Chapter 5: Game Mechanics and Scoring System

5.1 Movement and Shooting Basics

Movement Controls

- **Early Stages (Classic Mode):** Movement is restricted to left and right, similar to the original *Space Invaders*.

- **Mid-Game Evolution:** Unlocks **vertical movement**, allowing for more strategic positioning.

- **Advanced Evolution:** Enables **full 360-degree movement**, turning the game into a dynamic bullet-hell shooter.

Shooting Mechanics

- **Basic Laser:** Fires a single shot at a time; later upgrades allow multiple projectiles.

- **Auto-Fire:** Can be toggled on for rapid shooting, helpful in bullet-heavy sections.

- **Charge Shots:** Some weapons require charging before releasing a **high-damage blast**.

- **Directional Shooting:** In later stages, some ships can fire in multiple directions simultaneously.

Dodging and Positioning

- Staying in **constant motion** reduces the risk of getting hit.

- Positioning near the **edges of the screen** allows for quick dodging.

- Some ships have **smaller hitboxes**, making it easier to weave through enemy fire.

5.2 Scoring Multipliers and Bonus Points

Base Scoring System

- Each **enemy defeated** grants a base point value.

- Stronger enemies and **bosses** give **higher score rewards**.

- Destroying enemies **quickly** increases the point value.

Scoring Multipliers

Multipliers are essential for achieving **high scores** and unlocking additional game content.

Multiplier Type	Effect	How to Trigger
Combo Multiplier	Increases score as enemies are destroyed consecutively	Kill enemies without missing shots

Speed Bonus	Extra points for clearing waves quickly	Defeat enemies as soon as they appear
No-Hit Bonus	Large point bonus at the end of a stage	Complete a level without taking damage
Perfect Accuracy Bonus	Extra points for hitting every shot	Avoid missing any shots in a wave
Boss Takedown Bonus	Additional points for quick boss defeats	Eliminate a boss under a time limit

Bonus Point Opportunities

- **Hidden Enemies:** Some levels feature **secret enemies** that grant large score bonuses.

- **Chain Kills:** Destroying **multiple enemies at once** (with explosions or spread shots) grants **extra points**.

- **Stage Completion Rank:** Stages are graded based on performance (S, A, B, C ranks), rewarding **higher scores for better rankings**.

5.3 Special Abilities and Power-ups

As the game evolves, players gain access to **special abilities** and power-ups that **enhance combat and survival**.

Special Abilities

Ability	Effect	How to Unlock
Hyper Mode	Temporarily increases fire rate and damage	Earned by defeating mid-game bosses
Time Slow	Slows enemy movements for easier dodging	Found in later stages
Energy Burst	Releases a screen-clearing explosion	Gained through Evolution Upgrades
Shield Generator	Blocks incoming damage for a short time	Power-up drop from enemies
Gravity Wave	Pushes enemies away, disrupting their attacks	Unlockable via high score achievements

Power-ups

Power-ups drop **randomly from enemies or specific stage sections**.

Power-up	Effect
Rapid Fire	Temporarily increases fire rate
Double Shot	Allows two simultaneous shots instead of one

Spread Upgrade	Increases spread shot coverage
Homing Missiles	Adds homing missiles to your standard attacks
Invincibility Shield	Grants temporary immunity to damage

Using power-ups effectively can **turn the tide of battle**, especially during **challenging boss fights or enemy waves**.

5.4 Advanced Tactics for High Scores

For those aiming to reach **top leaderboard rankings**, using **advanced tactics** is essential.

1. Enemy Pattern Memorization

- Enemies follow **specific movement patterns**—learning these allows **preemptive dodging and faster kills**.

- Some enemies have **weak spots** that take more damage—targeting these speeds up fights.

2. Efficient Use of Power-ups

- Avoid using power-ups **immediately**—save them for **boss fights or tough waves**.

- Combining **multiple power-ups** (e.g., Rapid Fire + Spread Shot) **amplifies attack potential**.

3. Chain Combos for Maximum Multipliers

- Try to **eliminate multiple enemies quickly** without gaps in attacks.

- Avoid **missing shots**—every accurate hit increases the **combo multiplier**.

4. Boss Battle Strategies

- Most **bosses have different attack phases**—anticipate changes in patterns.

- Some **bosses drop extra score bonuses** if defeated **without taking damage**.

- **Focus fire on weak points** to speed up boss eliminations.

5. Risk vs. Reward Playstyle

- Playing aggressively by **staying near enemies** allows for **faster kills and higher scores**.

- However, it also **increases the risk of getting hit**—balance offense and defense wisely.

Chapter 6: Enemy Types and Attack Patterns

6.1 Classic Invaders and Their Behavior

The **original Space Invaders** return in *Infinity Gene Evolve*, but they gradually **evolve** into more aggressive versions as the game progresses.

Basic Classic Invaders:

Enemy Type	Behavior	Weakness
Standard Invader	Moves left and right, gradually descending	Single-shot elimination
Fast Invader	Moves quicker than standard enemies, drops faster at lower numbers	Predictable horizontal movement
Shielded Invader	Has a barrier that blocks one hit before taking damage	Wait for barrier cooldown, then attack
Shooting Invader	Fires slow-moving projectiles at the player	Stay mobile to avoid shots
Commander Invader	Buffs nearby invaders, making them faster	Target first to disable enemy speed boost

Behavioral Patterns:

- **Enemies start slow but speed up as their numbers decrease**.

- Some **invaders reposition strategically** instead of descending in a straight line.

- Later stages introduce **multi-hit enemies that require stronger weapons** to defeat.

6.2 New Enemy Types Introduced in Evolve

As the game evolves, new **high-tech enemies** appear, bringing **advanced attack patterns** and **bullet-hell mechanics**.

New Enemy	Description	Attack Style	Strategy to Defeat
Phantom Invader	Transparent enemies that fade in and out	Becomes intangible periodically	Attack when visible
Swarm Drone	Small, fast-moving units in large groups	Charges at the player	Use spread shots for crowd control
Laser Sentinel	A large invader with rotating cannons	Fires continuous laser beams	Move between laser gaps

Teleport Invader	Warps to different screen locations	Fires homing projectiles	Dodge, then counterattack after teleport
Exploding Invader	Self-destructs when hit, damaging nearby enemies and the player	Explosion covers a large area	Attack from a safe distance

Evolutionary Behavior Changes:

- Enemies **adapt**—some gain **shields**, others **split into smaller forms** when destroyed.

- Later enemies **fire energy waves, lasers, and homing missiles**.

- **Swarm behavior becomes unpredictable**, requiring quick reactions.

6.3 Boss Battles and How to Defeat Them

Bosses in *Infinity Gene Evolve* feature **multi-phase battles**, requiring players to adapt their strategies.

Common Boss Traits:

- **Multiple Weak Points:** Some bosses require **targeting specific areas** to deal damage.

- **Phase Transitions:** Bosses change **attack styles mid-battle**, adding difficulty.

- **Environmental Hazards:** Some encounters have **moving obstacles or limited space.**

Notable Bosses & Strategies:

Boss Name	Appearance	Attack Pattern	Weakness
Gigaton Invader	A giant version of a classic invader	Fires massive energy blasts and spreads smaller invaders	Aim at the flashing core when it opens
Neon Swarm Core	A pulsating sphere with rotating shields	Shoots swarms of fast-moving drones	Destroy drones first to expose core
Quantum Warper	A shifting form that teleports across the screen	Shoots homing lasers after teleporting	Predict movement and fire ahead of time
Armored Colossus	A multi-segmented invader with reinforced plating	Unleashes shockwaves when hit	Target the glowing weak spots
Final Evolution Entity	The ultimate boss, shifting between multiple enemy forms	Combines all previous attack patterns	Adapt to form changes and dodge strategically

Boss Battle Tips:

- **Save special weapons** (like charge beams) for **weak-point exposure moments**.

- **Focus on survival**—bosses have **predictable patterns**, so patience is key.

- **Use power-ups wisely**—a shield or time slow can turn the tide in tough battles.

6.4 Surviving Swarm Attacks and Bullet Hell Sequences

In later stages, enemies **attack in massive numbers**, creating **bullet-hell situations**.

How Swarm Attacks Work:

- **Enemies flood the screen from multiple directions**.

- **Projectiles create complex bullet patterns**, forcing precise movement.

- **Some enemies split into multiple forms upon destruction**.

Best Strategies for Survival:

Tactic	How It Helps
Stay Mobile	Constant movement reduces the chance of being hit
Use the Whole Screen	Don't stay in one area—move up/down and side to side
Fire Continuously	Keeping up pressure prevents overwhelming enemy numbers
Memorize Attack Patterns	Bosses and enemies follow set sequences—learning them helps avoid damage
Use Power-Ups Smartly	Save shields or time slow for the hardest sections

Dodging Bullet Hell Sequences:

- **Look for gaps in bullet patterns**—not all attacks cover the whole screen.

- **Move with the rhythm of enemy fire**—many projectiles follow predictable waves.

- **Prioritize survival over attacking**—sometimes dodging is the best strategy.

Chapter 7: Game Modes and Challenges

7.1 Classic Mode vs. Evolution Mode

Classic Mode

- Inspired by the **original 1978 Space Invaders** gameplay.

- **Limited movement** (only left and right initially).

- Enemies descend **in fixed patterns** with increasing speed.

- **Single weapon type**—no upgrades or evolution.

- Best for players who **want a nostalgic experience**.

Evolution Mode

- Introduces **game evolution**, unlocking **new abilities, weapons, and movement styles**.

- Enemies **change forms, attack patterns, and increase in difficulty** over time.

- **Stages transition from 2D to 3D**, creating a dynamic experience.

- Features **multiple weapon types, power-ups, and special abilities**.

- Best for players who **want a progressive and evolving challenge**.

Key Differences

Feature	Classic Mode	Evolution Mode
Movement	Left and right only	Full 360-degree movement
Weapons	Basic laser	Unlockable weapon upgrades
Enemies	Fixed patterns	Adaptive, evolving threats
Graphics	Pixelated, retro style	Modern visuals, 2D-3D transformation
Game Progression	Static gameplay	Unlockable abilities and upgrades

7.2 Survival Mode Strategies

Overview

- The goal is to **survive as long as possible** against endless waves of enemies.

- Each wave **increases in difficulty**, introducing stronger enemies and faster attack patterns.

- **Limited power-ups**—players must manage resources wisely.

- High scores are **based on survival time and enemy destruction**.

Survival Tips:

1. Prioritize Movement Over Attacking

- Staying **constantly mobile** helps dodge increasing bullet patterns.

- Use **circular movement** to avoid getting cornered.

2. Manage Power-Ups Wisely

- Save **defensive power-ups** (shields, time slow) for later waves.

- Use **offensive power-ups** (spread shot, rapid fire) for enemy swarms.

3. Target Key Enemies First

- Eliminate **Commander Invaders** that boost enemy speed.

- Destroy **Exploding Invaders** from a distance to avoid self-damage.

4. Learn Enemy Wave Patterns

- **Early waves** are predictable—use them to build score multipliers.

- **Later waves** require quick adaptability—memorizing attack patterns is key.

7.3 Time Attack and Score Attack Tips

Time Attack Mode

- Players must **clear waves as quickly as possible** within a time limit.

- Higher **speed bonuses** are awarded for **faster eliminations**.

Strategies for Time Attack:

- **Use high-damage weapons** like laser beams to clear enemies instantly.

- **Positioning matters**—stay near **enemy spawn zones** to attack quickly.

- **Avoid unnecessary dodging**—aggression is rewarded in this mode.

Score Attack Mode

- The objective is to **get the highest score within a fixed time limit**.

- Multipliers are **crucial**—keeping a **perfect combo** is key.

Strategies for Score Attack:

- **Never break a combo**—missing shots reduces multipliers.

- **Destroy enemies in chains**—target groups for bonus points.

- **Use special abilities wisely**—activating **Hyper Mode** at peak multiplier gives maximum score.

7.4 Special Events and Limited-Time Challenges

Overview

- These **seasonal or special event** modes introduce **unique enemies, gameplay twists, and exclusive rewards**.

- Some events **restrict weapon types** or **introduce modified physics** (e.g., low gravity battles).

Event Types

Event Mode	Challenge Type	Rewards
Boss Rush	Defeat multiple bosses in a row	Rare ship unlocks
Hardcore Mode	Play with **one life only**	High-score leaderboard rankings
Weapon Challenge	Use a **specific weapon loadout only**	Special power-ups
Timed Survival	Survive for a set period against overwhelming waves	Bonus score multipliers

Tips for Special Events:

- **Practice event mechanics** before aiming for leaderboard rankings.

- **Adapt to restrictions**—some events remove auto-fire or limit movement.

- **Maximize event rewards**—many events offer **exclusive ship skins or power-ups**.

Chapter 8: Advanced Strategies and Pro Tips

8.1 Dodging and Positioning Techniques

Mastering Movement

- **Stay mobile** – Never remain in one spot for too long, as enemies adapt their attacks.

- **Use the edges wisely** – Moving towards screen edges can reduce threats from multiple sides.

- **Predict enemy fire** – Observe enemy patterns and pre-position yourself before attacks land.

Dodging Bullet Hell Patterns

- **Micro-dodging** – Instead of large movements, use **small precise shifts** to weave between bullets.

- **Pathfinding dodges** – Look for bullet gaps and plan a **safe path in advance**.

- **Circular dodging** – Moving in a **slow circle** helps avoid swarms of enemy projectiles.

Positioning for Maximum Offense

- **Stay mid-screen when possible** – Provides equal access to all enemy positions.

- **Use vertical movement** – Not just side-to-side; evolving enemies attack from multiple angles.

- **Corner strategy** – In later stages, controlled movement in corners helps control enemy waves.

8.2 Effective Weapon Usage and Combos

Weapon Types and Their Best Uses

Each weapon has **strengths and weaknesses**. Combining the right loadout **maximizes damage output**.

Weapon Type	Best For	Weakness
Spread Shot	Swarm control, covering wide areas	Weaker against single targets
Laser Beam	Piercing through multiple enemies	Slow recharge, bad for swarms
Homing Missiles	Hitting moving targets	Weaker direct damage
Charge Shot	High burst damage on bosses	Requires timing and aim

Rapid Fire	Continuous damage, good for close-range	Consumes energy quickly

Combining Weapons for Maximum Efficiency

- **Spread + Homing Missiles** – Covers large areas while locking onto priority targets.

- **Charge Shot + Laser** – Devastating against **boss weak points**.

- **Rapid Fire + Shield** – Aggressive playstyle that keeps up sustained damage while absorbing hits.

8.3 Exploiting Enemy Weaknesses

Targeting Weak Points

- Some enemies have **glowing cores—aim for these to destroy them faster**.

- **Multi-segment bosses** require **targeting specific sections first** to weaken them.

Enemy-Specific Exploits

Enemy Type	Weakness	Best Counter
Armored Invader	Takes less damage from front	Attack from above or below

Teleport Invader	Can't be hit while teleporting	Predict its movement and fire ahead
Exploding Drone	Destroys nearby enemies upon death	Use its explosion to clear groups
Shielded Sentinel	Blocks frontal attacks	Wait for shield cooldown or attack from behind

Using Enemy Waves to Your Advantage

- Destroying **certain enemies first** can **reduce enemy aggression**.

- Some enemies **trigger chain reactions—use explosions strategically**.

- Luring enemies into **tight formations** makes it easier to wipe them out in one move.

8.4 Speedrunning and High-Score Optimization

Speedrunning Tactics

- **Memorize enemy spawns** – Anticipate waves and pre-fire before they appear.

- **Optimize movement** – Reduce unnecessary dodging to save time.

- **Use the right weapons** – **Charge Shots** and **Laser Beams** can clear waves instantly.

- **Abuse enemy patterns** – Some enemies **don't attack if you position yourself correctly**.

Maximizing Your Score

- **Never break a combo** – Keeping a high streak is essential for leaderboard rankings.

- **Focus on multipliers** – Destroying enemies **quickly and efficiently** maximizes points.

- **Utilize power-ups strategically** – Activating **Hyper Mode** during boss fights yields the highest scores.

- **Destroy hidden bonus enemies** – Some stages have **secret targets** that award extra points.

Chapter 9: Secrets, Unlockables, and Easter Eggs

9.1 Hidden Features and Bonus Content

Unlockable Soundtracks

- The game features **remixed versions** of classic *Space Invaders* music.

- **Hidden tracks** can be unlocked by completing **specific challenges**.

Graphical Filter Options

- Players can unlock **retro visual styles** that replicate classic arcade aesthetics.

- Filters include **pixel art mode, vector-style wireframes, and CRT scanlines**.

Hidden Stages and Extra Missions

- Some levels contain **secret exits** leading to **bonus challenge stages**.

- Completing these hidden stages unlocks **extra difficulty settings and exclusive rewards**.

9.2 Unlocking Classic Space Invaders Modes

Classic 1978 Mode

- This mode replicates the **original arcade experience** with **authentic 2D graphics and fixed movement**.

- **How to unlock:** Defeat 500 classic invaders in Evolution Mode.

Monochrome Mode

- A black-and-white version of *Space Invaders*, mimicking **early arcade screens**.

- **How to unlock:** Complete any level using only the **default ship and weapon**.

Reverse Mode

- In this mode, **players control the invaders** and attack a stationary defense turret.

- **How to unlock:** Get an **A-rank** on 10 different levels.

9.3 TAITO Guest Ships and How to Get Them

What Are Guest Ships?

- *Infinity Gene Evolve* features **ships from other classic TAITO games**, each with unique abilities.

- These ships offer **alternative playstyles** compared to the default fighter.

Unlockable Guest Ships and How to Get Them

Ship	Game Origin	How to Unlock
Silver Hawk	*Darius*	Defeat a total of 5 bosses in Evolution Mode.
R-Gray 1	*RayStorm*	Complete a full Survival Mode run without dying.
X-Lay	*G-Darius*	Score over 1,000,000 points in Score Attack.
Metal Black Fighter	*Metal Black*	Destroy 500 enemies using Charge Shots.
Arkanoid Vaus	*Arkanoid*	Clear a special hidden stage featuring Arkanoid paddles.

Benefits of Using Guest Ships

- **Different weapon styles** – Some ships use **homing lasers, charge shots, or wide-area beams**.

- **Unique movement abilities** – Certain guest ships have **faster speed or defensive shields**.

- **Exclusive achievements** – Playing with guest ships unlocks **extra trophies and challenges**.

9.4 Secret Codes and Cheats

Unlockable Cheats and How to Activate Them

Some hidden codes allow **modifying gameplay mechanics**, similar to classic arcade cheat codes.

Cheat Code	Effect	How to Activate
"HYPERLASER"	Unlocks max-powered weapons	Enter as a player name
"OLDSCHOOL"	Enables **monochrome retro mode**	Press Up, Down, Left, Right, A at title screen
"INFINITE"	Grants unlimited lives (Practice Mode only)	Hold L1 + R1 while selecting a stage
"SLOWMO"	Enables bullet-time mode	Complete any level without firing a shot

"GUESTMODE"	Instantly unlocks all guest ships	Finish the game once on Hard Mode

Developer Easter Eggs

- Entering **"TAITO1978"** as a name **activates a secret developer message.**

- There is a **hidden boss fight** only accessible **on the final level under specific conditions.**

- Destroying **certain background objects** in some levels **reveals classic arcade sprites** from *Space Invaders, Arkanoid, and Darius.*

Chapter 10: Conclusion and Community Resources

10.1 Final Thoughts and Mastering the Game

Key Takeaways from the Guide

- **Understand Evolution Mechanics** – Progression in *Infinity Gene Evolve* is **not just about surviving** but **adapting** as the game transforms over time.

- **Master Dodging and Positioning** – Advanced bullet-dodging techniques like **micro-dodging, circular movement, and enemy wave prediction** will help you **survive longer and maintain score multipliers**.

- **Optimize Weapon Loadouts** – Each **weapon type suits different scenarios**. Learning **when to switch** between them is key to **maximizing efficiency**.

- **Exploit Enemy Weaknesses** – Recognizing **enemy patterns and weak points** can make even the hardest boss battles more manageable.

- **Explore and Unlock Hidden Features** – From **classic modes and guest ships to Easter eggs**, the game rewards **dedicated players** who experiment and explore.

Becoming a True Master

- **Practice Score Attack & Survival Mode** – To rank on global leaderboards, focus on **score multipliers, power-up management, and enemy wave memorization**.

- **Engage with the Community** – Learn from **top-tier players** by watching their runs, discussing strategies, and participating in competitions.

- **Speedrun Techniques** – If you aim to **beat the game as fast as possible**, study **speedrunning routes, enemy spawn timings, and high-damage weapon strategies**.

10.2 Best Online Forums and Discord Communities

Staying connected with the *Space Invaders* community allows players to **share high scores, discover new strategies, and discuss updates**. Below are some of the best **forums, Discord servers, and social platforms** to engage with fellow fans.

Top Online Communities

Platform	Description	Link/Access
Reddit - r/spaceinvaders	Community for discussing *Space Invaders*, posting high scores, and sharing tips.	reddit.com/r/spaceinvaders

TAITO Official Discord	The official TAITO server with discussions on *Infinity Gene Evolve* and other games.	Invite available via TAITO's website.
Shmups Forum	A community for shoot-'em-up (shmup) fans, with discussions on *Space Invaders* and similar games.	shmups.system11.org
Twitter & YouTube	Follow top players, developers, and tournament organizers for game updates.	Search **#SpaceInvadersEvolve**
Steam Community Hub	If playing on PC, this hub is great for finding **mods, updates, and multiplayer discussions**.	Steam store page.

How to Get the Most Out of These Communities

- **Post Your Gameplay** – Share **your best runs** and **ask for feedback** to improve.

- **Join Tournaments & Leaderboards** – Compete with **top players** to test your skills.

- **Stay Updated on Patches & DLC** – Developers **sometimes tweak difficulty and add new modes**, so keeping up-to-date is important.

- **Discuss Strategies & Find Co-Op Partners** – If the game introduces **multiplayer or co-op features**, these communities are the best place to find teammates.

10.3 Developer Insights and Future Updates

TAITO's Vision for Space Invaders Infinity Gene Evolve

TAITO has always been at the forefront of **arcade and shoot-'em-up (shmup) innovation**. With *Infinity Gene Evolve*, the developers aimed to create a game that **blends classic Space Invaders mechanics with modern evolution-based gameplay**.

Key Goals of Development:

- **Preserve nostalgia** – Keeping the essence of *Space Invaders* while evolving it for modern audiences.

- **Dynamic gameplay progression** – Introducing an **adaptive evolution system** that changes the way players experience each run.

- **Expanded weapon and ship customization** – Allowing players to **experiment with loadouts and guest ships**.

Upcoming Features and Speculated Updates

Based on **developer interviews, patch notes, and player feedback**, future updates may introduce:

- **New Evolution Phases** – More **graphical and gameplay transitions** as players progress.

- **Additional Ships and Weapons** – Potential guest fighters from **other TAITO franchises**.

- **New Game Modes** – Possible additions like **a roguelike mode or online multiplayer challenges**.

- **Special Events & Limited-Time Stages** – Seasonal events, **boss rushes, or community challenges**.

To stay up to date on **official announcements**, follow:

- **TAITO's Official Website & Social Media**

- **Steam or Console Patch Notes**

- **Gaming News Outlets Covering Arcade & Shmups**

10.4 FAQs and Troubleshooting

Frequently Asked Questions

Q: How do I unlock all game modes?

- Most modes unlock through **natural progression** or by achieving **high ranks** on multiple stages.

- **Classic 1978 Mode:** Defeat **500 classic invaders** in Evolution Mode.

- **Reverse Mode:** Get an **A-rank** in at least **10 different levels**.

Q: What's the best weapon for high scores?

- **Laser Beam + Homing Missiles** is a strong combo for **both clearing enemies quickly and targeting bosses efficiently**.

- **Charge Shot** is great for **maximizing damage while maintaining combo multipliers**.

Q: Are there cheat codes or hidden commands?

- Yes! Codes like **"HYPERLASER"** (max weapons) or **"OLDSCHOOL"** (monochrome mode) can be entered for extra fun. Check **Chapter 9.4** for a full list.

Q: Does the game support multiplayer or co-op?

- As of now, *Infinity Gene Evolve* is **single-player only**, but future updates **may introduce online leaderboards or challenges**.

Troubleshooting Common Issues

Issue	Solution
Game crashes on startup	Ensure your **graphics drivers are updated** and **verify game files** (Steam/console settings).
Input lag or slow response	Try **lowering graphics settings** and enabling **performance mode** (on PC/console).

Can't unlock a specific ship	Make sure you're **fulfilling the exact unlock requirements** (e.g., high scores, stage completion).
Sound glitches or missing audio	Restart the game, **check audio settings**, and ensure **your device drivers are up to date**.
Game not saving progress	Check if your **cloud save or local storage has space** and ensure **autosave is enabled**.

If the problem persists, visiting **official forums or the TAITO support page** can help with additional fixes.